WILLIAM McKINLEY

ENCYCLOPEDIA
of PRESIDENTS

William McKinley

Twenty-Fifth President of the United States

By Zachary Kent

Consultant: Charles Abele, Ph.D.
Social Studies Instructor
Chicago Public School System

CHILDRENS PRESS ®

CHICAGO

**William McKinley,
twenty-fifth president
of the United States**

Library of Congress Cataloging-in-Publication Data

Kent, Zachary.
  William McKinley / by Zachary Kent.
      p.   cm. — (Encyclopedia of presidents)
  Includes index.
  Summary: Presents the early life, military career, and
political life of the president who was assassinated in 1901
during his second term in office.
  ISBN 0-516-01361-0
  1. McKinley, William, 1843-1901 — Juvenile
literature. 2. Presidents — United States — Biography —
Juvenile literature.   3.   United States — History — War of
1898 — Juvenile literature.   4.   United States — -Politics and
government — 1897-1901 — Juvenile literature. [1. McKinley,
William, 1843-1901. 2. Presidents.] I. Title. II. Series.
E711.6.K46   1988
973.8'8'0924 — dc19   88-10881
[B]   CIP
[92]   AC

Picture Acknowledgments

AP/Wide World Photos — 9, 29, 50, 68, 73, 84,
88 (2 photos)

The Bettmann Archive — 4, 10, 17, 21, 33, 34,
52, 65, 77, 86, 87

Historical Pictures Service, Chicago — 5, 12, 16,
19, 22, 23, 24, 25, 26, 36, 39, 42, 46, 48, 53, 57,
59, 61, 63, 67, 70, 74, 76, 78, 81, 82, 85

Courtesy Library of Congress — 6, 15, 31, 32, 49,
51, 54, 56, 89 (2 photos)

North Wind Picture Archives — 37

Courtesy U.S. Bureau of Printing and
Engraving — 2

Cover design and illustration
by Steven Gaston Dobson

Childrens Press®, Chicago
Copyright ©1988 by Regensteiner Publishing Enterprises, Inc.
All rights reserved. Published simultaneously in Canada.
Printed in the United States of America.
1 2 3 4 5 6 7 8 9 10 R 97 96 95 94 93 92 91 90 89 88

The McKinleys in Canton, Ohio, during his first presidential campaign

Table of Contents

Chapter 1

Tragedy in Buffalo

Thousands of people swarmed the fairground of the Pan-American Exposition in Buffalo, New York, on September 6, 1901.

Outside a building called the Temple of Music, they jammed together excitedly, hoping to glimpse twenty-fifth U.S. president William McKinley. Early arrivals waited in line for a special chance to greet the popular president and even shake his hand.

Inside the Temple of Music, strains of classical music softly floated from a huge pipe organ. Officials and guards trotted past potted plants, stands of flowers, and rows of chairs as they made final preparations. At one end of the room on a raised platform stood President McKinley, looking stout, well-dressed, and dignified.

The day before, fifty thousand visitors had crowded the Exposition to listen as he gave an important speech on America's role in the world. But on this day the fifty-eight-year-old politician simply looked forward to meeting the public and shaking hands.

McKinley's personal secretary, George Cortelyou, worried about the president's safety. Earlier he had urged McKinley to cancel the reception. "Why should I?" calmly asked the president. "No one would wish to hurt me." Only ten minutes was planned for the event, and Cortelyou next argued that some of the waiting people might be upset if they did not get to shake his hand. "Well," the president answered kindly, "they'll know I tried, anyhow." Anxiously the loyal secretary positioned extra Secret Service men and city police detectives to watch out for danger during the reception.

Promptly at four o'clock McKinley nodded and said, "Let them come in." The doors were opened and the waiting throng pushed inside. Attendants kept the people moving slowly forward on a receiving line. The president smiled pleasantly and greeted each person as he or she approached. He showed special friendliness to the shy ones and to the little children. With each person he lightly shook hands, using his famous "McKinley grip" to prevent soreness in his fingers and blisters on his palms.

It was a very warm day and many people mopped perspiration from their faces with handkerchiefs. At 4:07 George Cortelyou signaled for the doors to be closed and no more people admitted. Just then a young, clean-shaven man in a black suit stepped up to meet the president. This Detroit mill worker named Leon Czolgosz wore a white handkerchief wrapped around his right hand as if it were a bandage. Concealed beneath the handkerchief he grasped a short-barreled .32 caliber Iver Johnson revolver. No one guessed that Czolgosz had come to kill the president.

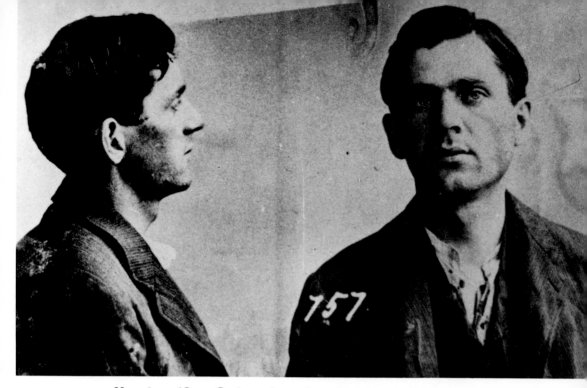

Mug shot of Leon Czolgosz from the police report of his crime

Standing face-to-face with the young man, McKinley reached out to shake his hand. Czolgosz lurched forward, and suddenly the sound of two gunshots sharply cracked the air. The president rose on his toes and stared in astonishment. Gray gunsmoke curled from a hole in Czolgosz's handkerchief. McKinley shivered and staggered backward into the arms of a Secret Service agent. Stunned bystanders jumped upon the assassin and roughly knocked him to the floor. As the president was led to a chair, the hand he clutched to his vest glistened with blood.

The music abruptly stopped and women screamed. Shouting people rushed to the exits to spread word of the awful shooting. The police dragged Czolgosz into the middle of the room.

"Don't let them hurt him," called out McKinley with pity when he saw these guards punch the captured man.

George B. Cortelyou, McKinley's personal secretary

Men stood fanning the stricken president with their hats as George Cortelyou rushed to his side. McKinley raised his bloodied hand and whispered, "My wife,—be careful, Cortelyou, how you tell her—oh be careful."

Within minutes McKinley was carried outside to the Exposition's electric powered ambulance. The crowds fell back and stared in shock as the car hummed forward to the fairground's small emergency hospital. Still thinking of the gunman, McKinley sighed, "It must have been some poor misguided fellow." At 4:18 doctors and nurses lay the president upon an operating table. As they undressed him one bullet dropped out of his clothes. Apparently deflected by a button, it had only grazed his ribs. The second bullet, however, had ripped deep within his abdomen. "I am in your hands," McKinley softly told the doctors as they hurriedly prepared to operate.

Across the country news of the attempted assassination clicked over telegraph wires. Dazed Americans clutched newspapers with the giant headlines, "PRESIDENT MCKINLEY SHOT!" Few people could believe that such a terrible thing was possible. William McKinley ranked among the most kindly and gentle men in the United States. Surely no one in the nation loved peace more than he did. Now he had fallen victim to a crazed assassin.

People hoped and prayed the president would survive his injury. Although unable to find and remove the bullet, the doctors voiced optimism. They moved him to a private home in Buffalo. "No serious symptoms have developed," a medical bulletin assured the worried public the next day. McKinley rested comfortably as Vice-President Theodore Roosevelt and members of the cabinet hurriedly arranged travel plans to visit him. As the new week began the doctors released other notices. On Monday they announced, "More and more satisfactory"; on Tuesday, "The most comfortable night since the attempt on his life." Wednesday brought the news, "Continues to gain."

Soon, however, McKinley took a turn for the worse. He grew feverish and doctors realized a general infection, deadly gangrene, had developed in his wound. Tearful friends and family gathered at his bedside. His condition lapsed beyond the skills of the doctors. Shortly after 2:15 on the morning of September 14, 1901, weeping citizens walked away from telegraph offices after hearing the doctors' brief bulletin: "The President is dead."

A lifetime of public duty to the nation had brought President William McKinley to his final peace.

Chapter 2

Ohio Boyhood

In the early 1840s the country town of Niles, Ohio, boasted little more than a dusty street, shaded by trees and lined by clapboard houses and a small church. The village grocery store occupied the lower part of a two-story house that had a brick chimney and ivy growing from the roof. Inside this simple house William McKinley, Jr., was born on January 29, 1843, the seventh of nine children in the large McKinley family. McKinley's father, William McKinley, Sr., managed the iron foundry in town. Its red-hot blast furnace refined iron into heavy bars. His mother, Nancy Allison McKinley, possessed a kindly character. She was deeply religious, and neighbors long remembered her services of charity to the sick and poor in the village.

Of Scotch heritage, the hardworking McKinleys were strict but loving toward their children. While William was still a little boy, his parents assigned him household chores like chopping wood and driving the family cows to pasture. Mrs. McKinley observed that her son was often quiet. Rather than talk, he preferred to watch and listen to people. "He began to take notice of things when very young," his mother later recalled.

Opposite page: William McKinley
at the age of fifteen

The McKinleys insisted that all their children get an education. "I put my children in school just as early as they could go alone to the teacher," remembered Mrs. McKinley. William enjoyed attending the public school. In the one-room wooden schoolhouse he learned reading, writing, and arithmetic. "Billy had a head on his shoulders," remarked one of his teachers later.

Out of doors he showed his energy and spirit for fun. When the United States was at war with Mexico, from 1846 to 1848, William and his playmates got caught up in the patriotic excitement. Wearing paper hats and carrying wooden swords, they marched around and played at war. In the winters William tied blades to his shoes and ice-skated. In the summers he fished with hook and line, and once he almost drowned while swimming in local Mosquito Creek. As for games, his mother recalled, "William was a great hand for marbles and he was very fond of his bow and arrow and could hit almost anything that he aimed at. . . . He was just like other boys, except that he was of a more serious turn of mind."

To assure their children a better chance at learning, in 1852 the McKinleys moved ten miles south to the larger town of Poland, Ohio. Their new house was a large white frame dwelling with maple trees in the yard and a white picket fence. After attending the local public school for a time, nine-year-old William next attended the Poland Academy, where he threw himself into his studies.

"He was always studying, studying, studying all the time," one friend later remembered. "It was seldom that his head was not in a book," another classmate recalled.

14

The birthplace of William McKinley in Niles, Ohio

Baseball, camping, and kite-flying filled some of the teenager's free time. But as he grew older, what he enjoyed the most was taking part in the academy's debate society. In a special clubroom he and other students discussed literature, history, and philosophy. Sometimes they debated about slavery in the southern states, which was threatening to tear the North and South in two.

In the fall of 1860 seventeen-year-old McKinley packed a trunk and headed into Pennsylvania. With family savings the young man enrolled at Allegheny College in Meadville. His mother hoped he would study to become a Methodist minister. But McKinley worked so hard at his studies that he fell ill. Sickness and money troubles at home forced him to drop out after only a few months.

15

William McKinley, Sr., father of the president

An uncle had left McKinley's father with his debts. As soon as he regained his health, William determined to find a job to help the family during its hard times. If he earned enough, he expected he could someday return to college. He applied for a vacant teaching position in Poland's Kerr district school and was hired. The schoolhouse stood three miles outside of town. Every day the slim, handsome young teacher walked the whole distance, jumping fences and tramping across lots and fields. "My wages were, I think $25 a month, and I boarded around," McKinley later remarked. "My parents, however, lived only three miles from the schoolhouse, and most of the time I stayed with them and walked to school and back every day."

The cover picture on a Lincoln campaign song

After the school session ended, McKinley next found a position as a clerk in the Poland post office. Most likely he sorted mail, sold stamps, and dusted the shelves. While he performed these tasks, perhaps he calmly planned for his future education. But in the spring of 1861 national events suddenly changed the young man's life.

The 1860 election of Abraham Lincoln as sixteenth U.S. president angered many southern slaveowners. They feared that Lincoln would abolish slavery. Rather than submit, eleven slave states quit the Union and formed the Confederate States of America. In April 1861, Confederate cannon bombarded Fort Sumter in the harbor of Charleston, South Carolina, forcing the surrender of the U.S. garrison. The next day Lincoln called upon loyal troops to put down the rebellion. The American Civil War had begun.

17

At a Poland town meeting in June 1861, farmers and merchants filled the streets and pledged to fight for the Union. Children waved flags and people cheered as patriotic townsmen volunteered to serve in a new company to be called the Poland Guards. Later in the day McKinley discussed the situation with his cousin, William Osborne. "Bill, we can't stay out of this war," McKinley exclaimed. "We must get in." The two went to McKinley's house and told Mrs. McKinley of their decision to enlist. "Well, boys, if you think it is your duty to fight for your country," she quietly replied, "I think you ought to go."

At Camp Chase near Columbus, Ohio, the eager Poland Guard recruits joined the Twenty-Third Ohio Volunteer Infantry Regiment and became part of the U.S. Army. In camp these new soldiers received their blue uniforms and learned to march in formation and shoot muskets. In a letter home, eighteen-year-old Private McKinley exclaimed, "Our boys are all determined to stand by the stars and stripes, and never give up. . . ."

The end of July 1861 found the regiment marching south into the mountains of present-day West Virginia. For several weeks McKinley and his comrades guarded the region against Confederate raiders. They never spotted the enemy, although on one dark night McKinley's lieutenant swung his sword at a skunk. "We came to this conclusion," joked McKinley, "from the fact that a strong smell issued from the bushes."

On September 10, 1861, the Twenty-Third Ohio Regiment encountered the enemy for the first time at the Battle of Carnifex Ferry, West Virginia. As Union officers

McKinley at the time of his enlistment in the army

barked orders the enlisted men tramped forward. McKinley remembered, "the firing commenced, and . . . the booming of cannon . . . could be distinctly heard, and the smoke could be seen rising to the Heavens." Private McKinley stumbled ahead through thickets and across cornfields, shooting his gun. At the end of the day's confusion the Confederates retreated.

"This was our first real fight," McKinley later declared, "and the effect of the victory was of far more consequence to us than the battle itself. It gave us confidence in ourselves and faith in our commander. We learned that we could fight and whip the rebels on their own ground."

During the winter of 1861 to 1862 McKinley's regiment skirmished with the gray-clad Confederates twice more. Most of their time, however, the soldiers spent in camp. In the cold weather they performed guard duty, played cards, and wrote letters home. Finally in April 1862 fresh orders arrived. Soon the soldiers of the Twenty-Third Ohio rattled eastward by train to Washington, D.C., where they joined the Union's great Army of the Potomac.

That April McKinley received his first promotion. As a commissary (mess) sergeant, McKinley performed many tiresome duties. He distributed food rations to hungry troops and also saw that the regiment's horses received their fodder to eat. He personally supervised the transportation and unloading of supplies and handled the paperwork connected with it. He checked columns of numbers, counted barrels of food, and weighed sacks of grain. Watching McKinley go about his daily work, Lieutenant Colonel Rutherford B. Hayes became impressed by the young sergeant. Proudly Hayes later noted, "We soon found that in business, in executive ability, young McKinley was a man of rare capacity, especially for a boy of his age."

On September 17, 1862, the Army of the Potomac clashed with General Robert E. Lee's Confederate army at Sharpsburg, Maryland. In the bloodiest single day of the Civil War, blue and gray troops fought savagely along the banks of Antietam Creek. Guarding supply wagons behind the Union lines, Sergeant McKinley heard the roaring noise of the battle. He knew the men of his regiment were suffering and dying. Anxious to help his friends at the

The Civil War battle at Sharpsburg, Maryland

front, late in the afternoon McKinley quickly prepared a
wagon. Climbing aboard, he whipped the mules and
dashed forward to the battle line. One soldier of the Twenty-Third Ohio later declared, "Our Regiment had gone
into the fight at daylight, without breakfast . . . of any
kind, and was . . . almost completely exhausted from
fighting, fatigue, and lack of food and water. While in this
condition we saw a wagon, drawn by army mules, coming
towards us from the rear at breakneck speed, through a
terrific fire of musketry and artillery. . . . I have many
times since thought it a miracle that it . . . was not utterly
destroyed. The wagon, when it arrived, proved to be in
charge of Comrade McKinley, and contained a supply of
cooked rations, meat, coffee, and hardtack, and was hearti-
ly welcomed by our tired and half famished boys."

McKinley at age nineteen, as a second lieutenant

Colonel Hayes later exclaimed, "From his hands every man in the regiment was served with hot coffee and warm meats, a thing that had never occurred under similar circumstances in any other army in the world." As a result of this act of bravery at the Battle of Antietam, McKinley received a promotion to the rank of second lieutenant. When he visited home that fall on a furlough, the nineteen-year-old proudly wore the golden shoulder straps that marked him as an officer.

During 1863 and 1864 McKinley had many opportunities to display his worth. Promoted to first lieutenant in March 1863, he helped chase John Morgan's rebel raiders in Ohio and later fought at the Battle of Cloyd's Mountain. July 24, 1864, found the Twenty-Third Ohio and other Union regiments surprised by Southern troops near Kernstown in Virginia's Shenandoah Valley.

Union troops under enemy fire

As the battle raged, Colonel Hayes spied a nearby Union regiment in danger of being surrounded. Lieutenant McKinley immediately volunteered to save it. Bravely he spurred his little chestnut mare into a gallop. "We watched him push his horse through the open fields, over fences, through ditches," exclaimed Colonel Hayes, "while a well-directed fire from the enemy was poured upon him, with shells exploding around, about and over him." Finally out of the smoke the young lieutenant emerged, leading the stranded regiment to safety. Colonel Hayes afterwards grasped McKinley's hand and tearfully revealed, "I never expected to see you in life again."

The Army of the Potomac encamped at Cumberland Landing on the Pamunky River

For his outstanding courage McKinley was rewarded the next day with a promotion to captain. Colonel Hayes valued him highly and looked upon him almost as a son. Other officers, however, discovered a need for McKinley's services also. Before the spring of 1865 Captain McKinley saw fighting at Opequon and Cedar Creek, Virginia, and performed important duties on the staffs of Union generals George Crook and Winfield S. Hancock. Time and time again McKinley showed intelligence and daring. With satisfaction, Hayes, now a general himself, noted of McKinley, "Everyone admires him as one of the bravest and finest young officers in the army."

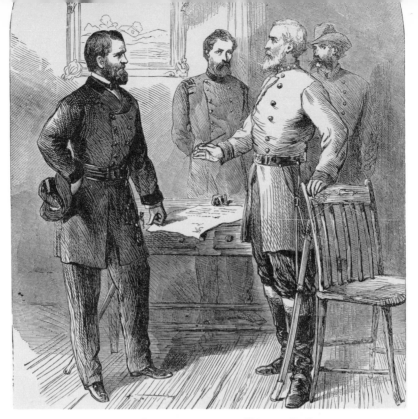

Robert E. Lee surrenders to Ulysses S. Grant

In April 1865, after four hard years of war, the weary Confederate armies collapsed. Confederate general Robert E. Lee surrendered to Union general Ulysses S. Grant at Appomattox Court House, Virginia, on April 9. The Union had won. The North and South were reunited as one nation again, and slavery was abolished. Union soldiers cheered throughout their camps and joyfully threw their hats into the air. Surely McKinley joined the celebrations, glad to know he had done his part. In March President Lincoln had promoted him to the brevet, or honorary, rank of major. Years later an Ohio army comrade was asked about McKinley's military career. "Why," the grizzled trooper simply explained, "he did what the rest of us did. Never shirked his duty. He was a good square fellow."

Chapter 3

The Young Napoleon

The Civil War's ugly scars would take many generations to heal. Throughout the North and South, however, the summer of 1865 found families welcoming uniformed sons and husbands home at last. By a miracle McKinley had survived the war without suffering from illness or receiving a single scratch. In addition, four years of camp life and battlefields had greatly matured him. "I was but a school-boy when I went into the army," he admitted. Now he returned to Poland, Ohio, a robust and muscular young man.

For a time the twenty-two-year-old major considered making the army his career. In the end, however, he chose to become a lawyer. The young veteran started his studies in the Youngstown, Ohio, law office of Charles Glidden. Hour after hour McKinley read law books and worked as a clerk. Greatly impressed by McKinley's abilities, Glidden urged him to attend a law school.

Opposite page: Major William McKinley
at the age of twenty-two

In the fall of 1866 the young major packed his bags and traveled to Albany, New York, to enter the Albany Law School. His roommate, George Arrel, remembered, "He was jolly, always good-natured, and looked at the bright side of everything. . . . Even at that time he had made up his mind to enter public life, and clearly showed an ambition to go to Congress." Before finishing the course of study, McKinley felt himself ready to practice law. He left school and in March 1867 he successfully passed his Ohio bar examinations.

Poland was too small a town in which to practice law. Instead McKinley opened an office in the city of Canton, Ohio, where his older sister was already a schoolteacher. McKinley's legal knowledge soon attracted the attention of respected Canton attorney Judge George W. Belden.

One evening Belden entered McKinley's office and dropped a sheaf of legal papers on his desk. A lawsuit was due to start in court the next day, but Belden claimed he did not feel well enough to present it. "If you don't try this case," he told McKinley, "it won't be tried." All that night the young lawyer studied the documents and prepared to appear in court for the very first time.

Canton lawyer William A. Lynch remembered observing McKinley in the courtroom: "Young, eager, ambitious, well-prepared, self-poised, but not over-confident; how he impressed me as he arose and told the court, 'What we contend for in this lawsuit'—I recall the very words of his opening."

McKinley argued his case successfully. Watching from the back of the courtroom, Judge Belden decided to invite

Rutherford B. Hayes

the young lawyer to become his partner. Joining Belden's
established law firm assured McKinley plenty of work.
Judge William R. Day later commented upon McKinley's
skills as a lawyer. "In the trial of a case Major McKinley
gained the confidence of the jury by the fairness and courtesy of his conduct. . . ."

As a member of the Republican party, McKinley took an
active part in local politics. In 1868, Union general Ulysses
S. Grant ran for U.S. president and McKinley's old commander, General Rutherford B. Hayes, ran for governor of
Ohio. Gladly McKinley campaigned for both these men,
giving stirring speeches from tavern steps and at other
public meetings.

Grant and Hayes won their elections, and Republicans impressed by McKinley asked him to run for prosecuting attorney of Stark County. The Canton newspaper supported him as "a good lawyer and a fine orator." Although many Stark County citizens were Democrats, still McKinley won the 1869 election. As the county's lawyer he performed his duties well, but later lost a try for a second term by just 143 votes.

Love entered the young lawyer's life in the summer of 1869. At a picnic he met Miss Ida Saxton, a witty, lively young woman freshly graduated from a finishing school. The Saxton family was well-known and respected in Canton. Mr. Saxton owned the First National Bank of Canton and employed Ida as a cashier.

As McKinley grew attracted to her, he found reasons to visit the bank more often. "Oh, if you could have seen what a beauty Ida was as a girl," he later exclaimed. For her part, Ida knew of the major's brave army adventures and was impressed by his charming manners and his handsome looks. Soon a deep romance blossomed between the two. For several months the couple courted. Then one evening while on a moonlight carriage ride, he proposed and she accepted. McKinley invited his dear friends Governor and Mrs. Hayes to the wedding. In his letter to them he explained, "I think I am doing a good thing. Miss S. is everything I could hope for."

On January 25, 1871, twenty-seven-year-old William McKinley and twenty-three-year-old Ida Saxton walked arm-in-arm down the aisle of the First Presbyterian Church of Canton as man and wife. After a honeymoon in

The McKinley home in Canton, Ohio

New York, the loving couple returned to settle in Canton. Mr. Saxton presented the newlyweds with the gift of a house on North Market Street.

While McKinley attended to his legal affairs and continued to build political support, his wife kept their house in order. On Christmas day great joy filled the McKinleys' lives when a baby daughter they named Katherine was born. As little Katie grew, her parents showered her with love and attention. The young family reveled in happiness until tragedy struck in 1873. Saddened by the death of her mother, Ida McKinley fell into poor health. Not long afterwards she gave birth to a second baby girl, whom they named Ida, but the sickly child died within the year.

Ida Saxton McKinley

After the loss of both her mother and her baby, Ida suffered deep mental depression and finally a complete physical breakdown. Devotedly McKinley watched over his wife and nursed her. She never fully recovered, however. Sleepless, nervous, and weak, she sometimes fell unconscious with sudden fits of epilepsy.

The crowning blow to the couple occurred in 1876 when four-year-old Katie died of typhoid fever. Totally shattered, Ida McKinley clung to her husband more than ever. McKinley's own grief at the loss of his children was beyond words. But he masked his terrible sadness by throwing himself into politics.

The Grand National Republican Banner for 1876

In 1876 Rutherford B. Hayes received the Republican nomination to run for president. Naturally McKinley stumped all over Ohio, speaking in behalf of the man he so greatly admired. He also campaigned hard and won his district's Republican congressional nomination. Through the fall he chatted with farmers, addressed workers in local mills and factories, and shook hands with strangers on sidewalks and in barbershops. In November, district voters chose McKinley by 3,300 votes over his Democratic opponent. At the age of thirty-three McKinley was bound for Congress.

Rutherford B. Hayes accepts the presidency.

The McKinleys traveled to Washington, D.C., and established themselves in a hotel suite at the Ebbit House before Congress met in the fall of 1877. After the extremely close 1876 presidential election, an electoral commission finally decided that Rutherford B. Hayes had won the right to be president. President Hayes often invited McKinley to visit him at the White House. Five feet seven inches tall, McKinley stood straight and walked with a brisk, military step. His clean-shaven, handsome face and clear blue eyes gave a strong and favorable impression.

One day Justice John Harlan entered Hayes's White House office as McKinley was stepping out. "Mr. President, who is that?" asked Harlan curiously. "That's McKinley, of Ohio, one of our new Congressmen," answered Hayes. "Well," predicted Harlan, "keep your eye on the young man. He may be President some day."

McKinley's daily routine as a congressman included meeting with Ohio visitors in his office and answering mail. In the House of Representatives he presented petitions and voted on legislation. The young Republican voted in favor of Civil Service reform and supported full rights for the nation's freed blacks. The issue of the tariff, however, received the greatest part of McKinley's attention.

The tariff was a collection of U.S. import taxes on foreign products which was designed to protect American industries. Though many wondered why wealthy corporations needed such protection, Congressman McKinley deeply believed in it. He remembered from boyhood how his father complained that foreign competition hurt the iron industry.

"Reduce the tariff and labor is the first to suffer," McKinley proclaimed in an attack on a suggested law to lower the tariff. With careful preparation he presented facts and figures in the House of Representatives to support his position. Standing with a striking posture and speaking in his bold, clear voice, the Ohio congressman greatly impressed many of his listeners.

In time, however, inaction and delay kept the lower tariff proposal from passing into law. Afterwards the *Canton Repository* reported, "Mr. McKinley's constituents may well be proud of him and his efforts to save the industries of his district from the ruin that threatened them in this wicked tariff scheme." During his congressional career McKinley made himself the nation's leading expert on tariff laws.

The original "gerrymander," a beast named in 1812
for Massachusetts governor Elbridge Gerry

When his two-year term neared its end in 1878, McKinley prepared to run for Congress again. Ohio's ruling Democrats were eager to unseat McKinley. Therefore they changed the borders of the state's congressional districts in an effort to favor their candidates. This political trick, called "gerrymandering," left McKinley's new congressional district filled with Democrats. "The redistricting," McKinley later recalled, "was not in the interest of fairness, but to increase Democratic representation, in violation of every principle of fairness."

President James A. Garfield

In the rough campaign that followed, McKinley worked day and night. Of his hard efforts he wrote President Hayes, "I mean to deserve success, anyhow." No one could have been happier than Hayes when on election day McKinley won an upset victory over his Democratic opponent by 1,200 votes. "Oh, the good luck of McKinley," exclaimed the president. "He was gerrymandered out and then beat the gerrymander!"

In 1880 McKinley made another successful run for Congress, winning by a margin of over 3,500 votes. President Hayes chose not seek a second four-year term. Instead, McKinley welcomed the presidential election of another Ohio friend, Congressman James A. Garfield. When President Garfield was tragically assassinated later that year, it was McKinley who arranged the memorial service in the House of Representatives.

In 1882 McKinley fought his toughest reelection race to date. The ballot count revealed that he had won by only eight votes. His opponent, Jonathan Wallace, challenged the count. After lengthy investigation, a congressional committee finally awarded the election to Wallace. In embarrassment, on May 27, 1884, McKinley gave up his seat and returned to Canton.

This defeat stung McKinley deeply, and for a time he wondered about his future. When someone asked him what he thought of politics as a career, he answered, "Before I went to Congress I had $10,000 and a practice worth $10,000 a year. Now I haven't either." Soon he regained his confidence, though, and loyal district Republicans rallied around him. In November 1884, by a majority of 2,000 votes, they put him back in office.

During the next two congressional elections McKinley won his campaigns by comfortable margins. In the House of Representatives the Ohioan's smooth, gentle manners and detailed political knowledge contributed to his rising reputation. McKinley also put in long office hours and once explained to his family in Ohio, "I have not written to you because first I have been up to my eyes with work." When teased about working too hard he laughed, "A good soldier must always be ready for his duty."

As a politician McKinley knew how to make friends out of enemies. In the halls and cloakrooms of the Capitol he was a familiar figure, warmly shaking hands, trading jokes, and exchanging ideas. Maine congressman Tom Reed commented with admiration, "McKinley was a great peace-maker." Robert La Follette of Wisconsin recalled,

McKinley in 1890, as chairman of the Ways and Means Committee

"He had a rare tact as a manager of men." His election to the chairmanship of the House's powerful Ways and Means Committee in 1889 added to his image as a leader.

It was perhaps as a public speaker, however, that McKinley made his greatest mark. When he was campaigning in Ohio and on national tours, people traveled for miles to listen to his vibrant words. In Congress, ladies crowded into the galleries on days when they knew he would speak. Standing short, handsome, and with a hand thrust into his coat, he quickly earned the nickname "The Young Napoleon." Congressman La Follette revealed, "McKinley was a magnetic speaker; he had a clear, bell-like quality of voice, with a thrill in it. He spoke with dignity, but with freedom of action. The pupils of his eyes would dilate until they were almost black, and his face, naturally without much color, would become almost like marble—a strong face, and a noble head."

McKinley called upon all of his political skills in a constant effort to maintain a high protective tariff. Some Democratic congressmen wished to lower the import taxes on certain items, including wool, in 1888. Congressman Leopold Morse of Massachusetts, who owned a clothing store, complained that American workingmen could not buy a woolen suit of clothes for ten dollars because of the high import tax on wool.

Soon after Morse voiced his complaint, McKinley rose from his seat with a bundle under his arm. Ripping the paper away he produced a woolen coat, vest, and trousers, along with a store bill for ten dollars.

Congressman Morse was quite skeptical of McKinley's ploy. He demanded to know where the Ohio congressman had bought the clothes. Smiling, McKinley answered, "Come now, will the gentleman from Massachusetts know his own goods?" The chamber echoed with laughter as members realized that McKinley had purchased the suit in Morse's own store.

Presenting facts and figures in convincing arguments, McKinley helped keep the tariff high. "The Republicans are loud in their praise of Major McKinley's leadership," reported one Washington newspaper. "They say he is cool, level headed and courageous, quick to see a point and alert in pressing it home."

In 1890 McKinley submitted legislation in the House that was designed to push the tariff upward. "It is framed in the interest of the people of the United States," he explained. "It is for the better defense of American homes and American industries."

During the House debate on the McKinley Tariff, its author seemed to be everywhere at once, coaxing congressmen for support and making compromises. A tax on imported tin, he insisted for example, would help create a whole new tin industry in the United States. At last Congress passed the McKinley Tariff, which taxed nearly four thousand different import items. On October 1, 1890, President Benjamin Harrison signed it into law.

Feeling that his greatest work as a congressman was finished, McKinley returned to Ohio to start his 1890 campaign for reelection. Once again the Democrats had gerrymandered McKinley's district to his disadvantage. The forty-seven-year-old veteran congressman rolled up his sleeves and threw himself into the campaign battle. "I can win," he cheerfully predicted. He realized, however, that he faced an uphill fight.

Surprisingly, the McKinley Tariff had backfired. No longer having to compete with foreign products, many American companies had raised the prices of their own products. On election day U.S. citizens, angered at these new expenses, took out their frustrations on the Republican party.

A count of the vote in McKinley's district revealed his defeat by 303 votes. At his headquarters loyal campaign workers sat completely stunned. George Frease, the editor of the *Canton Repository*, sadly looked at McKinley and muttered, "It's all over. What am I to say in the paper?" For a moment McKinley puffed on a cigar and then he hopefully responded, "In the time of darkest defeat, victory may be nearest."

Chapter 4

"We Want Yer, McKinley"

McKinley refused to let his defeat overcome him. Still admired by many Ohioans, in 1891 he accepted the Republican nomination to run for governor. Through the autumn months he campaigned harder than ever. By carriage and train he conducted a whirlwind tour into every corner of the state. Speaking several times a day, he delivered dozens of speeches to cheering crowds. On election day, his tireless efforts paid off. He beat Democrat James Campbell by over 21,000 votes.

On January 11, 1892, McKinley took the oath as governor at the state capitol in Columbus. In his inaugural address he explained to Ohio legislators, "It is my desire to cooperate with you in every endeavor to secure a wise, economical and honorable administration. . . ."

Eagerly the governor started his new job. He quickly called for laws to insure greater safety in Ohio's factories and on its railroads. Ohio workingmen praised McKinley for laws that allowed them to form trade unions and peacefully strike for better working conditions. A new excise tax on corporations helped fill the state treasury and reduced the tax burdens of Ohio's common citizens.

The McKinleys lived in a comfortable hotel suite across the street from the capitol. The governor's kindly devotion to his wife soon became famous throughout the city. Each morning he stopped in the street and waved up to her window before walking to his office. Every afternoon at exactly three o'clock he interrupted his business and stepped to his office window. With his handkerchief he waved to Ida, who watched for his loving signal from her bedroom. McKinley spent every moment of his free time catering to the needs of his sickly wife. When he was at work, she filled her idle hours crocheting bedroom slippers. Over the years she made thousands of pairs, which she donated to charity.

As Ohio governor, McKinley's national reputation continued to grow. When the Republican national convention convened in Minneapolis, McKinley attended as a delegate. Because of his well-known fairness, his comrades soon elected him convention chairman. Although President Benjamin Harrison won renomination on the first ballot with 535 votes, the 182 votes McKinley received obviously pleased him. Many Republicans openly talked of making Governor McKinley their presidential candidate in 1896. One powerful Ohio businessman, Mark Hanna, had been impressed with McKinley for years. With his money and influence, Hanna set about creating a political organization to propel McKinley into the White House.

McKinley's political future never looked brighter. Then suddenly, in February 1893, he faced personal financial ruin. Robert Walker, a longtime friend, had needed money for his business. Without concern, McKinley gladly endorsed and guaranteed Walker's bank loan notes. When Walker's business failed, McKinley unexpectedly found himself responsible for $130,000 in loans. This giant sum of money plunged the governor into debt. "I have kept clear of entanglements all my life," groaned McKinley in despair. "Oh, that this should come to me now!"

He vowed to repay every penny he owed. He guessed, however, that this scandal meant the end of his political career. Instead, he discovered that people greatly sympathized with his plight. "The financial troubles of Governor McKinley," noted one Columbus newspaper, "will be learned with deep regret not only in Ohio but all over the country. He has been a liberal, kind hearted man and has always done more for others than for himself."

Mark Hanna hurried to the rescue. He established a trust fund for McKinley and collected contributions from industrialists who approved of McKinley's tariff policies. Old friends, Civil War comrades, and even strangers also mailed small gifts of money. Soon the trust fund was able to repay McKinley's outstanding debt.

Grateful to put this problem behind him, McKinley ran for governor again in 1893. Visiting almost all of Ohio's 88 counties, he delivered 130 speeches and shook thousands of hands. Clearly he recognized his political strength when Ohioans reelected him with a landslide majority of over 80,000 votes.

During his campaign the popular governor often wore a red carnation in his buttonhole for good luck. Later the Ohio legislature decided to make the red carnation the state's official flower.

Governor McKinley in 1893

McKinley's second term as governor proved less peaceful than the first. In 1894 thousands of Ohio coal miners threw down their picks and shovels and went on strike. In some cities, striking mobs stopped trains and threw rocks at sheriff's deputies. McKinley ordered out the National Guard to stop the violence. During other strikes in the state that spring, McKinley called out the troops again. "I do not care if my political career is not twenty-four hours long," he declared. "These outrages must stop if it takes every soldier in Ohio." When he later learned that many mining families in the Hocking Valley were on the verge of starvation, however, he showed his concern by sending trainloads of emergency food and supplies.

McKinley refused to run for reelection as governor in 1895. Instead he became a private citizen in order to prepare for the upcoming presidential campaign. "It is just plain Mr. McKinley of Canton now; but wait a little while," predicted the *Canton Repository*. During the next months McKinley traveled through seventeen states and delivered scores of speeches.

When Republican delegates gathered at their national convention in Saint Louis, Missouri, in June 1896, McKinley was clearly the front-runner for the presidential nomination.

Mark Hanna had organized well. Everywhere McKinley clubs marched in the streets, waved banners, and shouted slogans. Supporters hawked McKinley buttons and canes and passed out McKinley pamphlets and leaflets. On walls and telegraph poles McKinley's face appeared on posters. Young Republican Theodore Roosevelt looked around at Hanna's work and exclaimed, "He has advertised McKinley as if he were a patent medicine."

"The air is full of McKinley," declared another politician at the convention hall. When Ohio senator Joseph Foraker finally offered McKinley's name for nomination, the delegates responded with incredible yells and cheering. Newspaperman Murat Halstead reported that the noise sounded "like a storm at sea with wild, fitful shrieks of wind."

On the first ballot McKinley easily won the Republican party's presidential nomination. For the vice-presidential candidate the delegates chose loyal Republican Garret A. Hobart of New Jersey.

William Jennings Bryan and supporters at the Democratic convention

When Democratic politicians met in Chicago in July, Nebraska congressman William Jennings Bryan rose up and spoke for the South and West. Struggling farmers in these regions believed the wider circulation of silver coins would solve their economic problems. The Republicans, however, insisted on maintaining gold as the government's standard precious metal. In a stirring convention speech Bryan proclaimed, "You shall not press down upon the brow of labor this crown of thorns, you shall not crucify mankind upon a cross of gold!" On the fifth ballot excited Democrats picked Bryan to be their candidate.

An 1896 photograph of William Jennings Bryan

Many wealthy and middle-class Americans disapproved of Bryan's radical economic ideas. Only thirty-six years old and in vigorous health, Bryan decided to take his campaign directly to the common people. With tremendous energy he crisscrossed the nation, covering 18,000 miles. From train platforms and in auditoriums he gave fiery speeches calling for economic justice. In three months' time he addressed as many as five million people. Enemies called him a socialist, a revolutionary, and a madman. Those Democrats thrilled by this message, though, compared his campaign to a kind of religious crusade. They gave him the nicknames "Boy Orator of the Platte," "The Silver Knight of the West," and "The Great Commoner."

McKinley gives a front-porch campaign speech from his home in Canton, Ohio.

McKinley realized immediately that he could never compete with his opponent's exciting campaign style. "I might just as well put up a trapeze on my front lawn and compete with some professional athlete as go out speaking against Bryan," he admitted. Instead McKinley stayed at home and let the public come to him. Through the summer and fall hundreds of delegations, representing farmers, laborers, businessmen, war veterans, college students, and professionals, swarmed into Canton. Campaign bands tooted patriotic tunes and choruses sang special compositions like "We Want Yer, McKinley, Yes, We Do."

McKinley and running mate Garret Hobart on a campaign coat of arms

Local militiamen called the Canton Home Guard paraded each group of visitors through the town until they reached McKinley's house on North Market Street. McKinley stepped out onto his front porch and greeted each new gathering with cheerful dignity. In carefully prepared speeches he explained his political views. Many of his catchiest phrases were reprinted. Mark Hanna's Republican organization swamped the country with millions of McKinley pamphlets containing such mottoes as "Good money never made times hard."

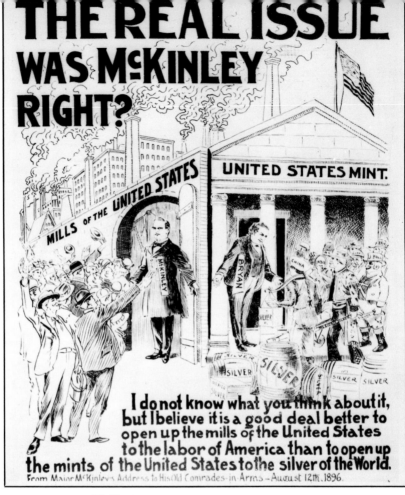

THE REAL ISSUE
WAS McKINLEY
RIGHT?

MILLS OF THE UNITED STATES

UNITED STATES MINT.

McKINLEY

BRYAN

CHINA

SILVER

SILVER

SILVER

SILVER SILVER

I do not know what you think about it, but I believe it is a good deal better to open up the mills of the United States to the labor of America than to open up the mints of the United States to the silver of the World.
From Major McKinley's Address to His Old Comrades-in-Arms – August 12th, 1896.

A pro-McKinley poster issued during his presidency

McKinley's front-porch campaign proved a great success. Visiting crowds yelled the popular Republican slogan "McKinley and the Full Dinner Pail" and groups of children sang, "Governor McKinley, he's our man; If we can't vote for him our papas can." Guests brought McKinley gifts of badges, canes, flags, flowers, cakes, cheeses, and even three caged eagles. Unfortunately, enthused crowds as large as 30,000 people often looked for souvenirs of their visits. Before long McKinley's picket fence was gone, his yard had turned to mud, and his porch was in danger of collapsing.

Nancy Allison McKinley, the president's mother

By election day some 750,000 people had visited Canton. On November 5, 1896, Americans across the country walked to their polling places to cast their votes. Through the day special telephone and telegraph lines brought the results to McKinley's Canton home. When all the votes were tallied they revealed:

	Popular Vote	Electoral Vote
William McKinley	7,108,480	271
William Jennings Bryan	6,511,495	176

By a comfortable margin, McKinley had been elected twenty-fifth president of the United States. That evening the major knelt with his wife and mother to give humble, prayerful thanks for his victory. Later he gladly received the telegram his dear friend Mark Hanna sent to him: "You are elected to the highest office of the land," it read, "by a people who always loved and trusted you."

Chapter 5

Remember the *Maine!*

The morning of March 4, 1897, dawned with clear skies and a mild breeze in Washington, D.C. At ten o'clock a troop of Ohio cavalry in handsome uniforms escorted fifty-four-year-old William McKinley to the White House. There he climbed into a waiting carriage with President Grover Cleveland. Together they wheeled down Pennsylvania Avenue past honor guards and cheering crowds. At the Capitol an even greater throng eagerly awaited the inauguration ceremony. Some men climbed trees and perched on branches in order to see better.

Americans in the 1890s felt strong, restless, and full of national pride. The country's hardy settlers had spent one hundred years taming the wilderness, plowing farms, and building factories. By 1897 the United States stretched all the way from Maine to California. Having filled the nation's natural boundaries, the people now wished to conquer new territories beyond the seas. "The taste of Empire is in the mouth of the people," the *Washington Post* exclaimed.

Opposite page: President and Mrs. McKinley in 1900   55

McKinley's wife and mother waiting to hear the inaugural address

Surely McKinley recognized the national feeling as he stepped onto the platform erected on the Capitol's east portico. While his wife and aged mother watched, McKinley placed his hand upon a Bible. Vowing to "preserve, protect and defend" the Constitution he took the oath of office as president. Then he turned to the crowd and delivered his inaugural address. "We want no wars of conquest," his voice rang out. "We must avoid the temptation of territorial aggression. War should never be entered upon

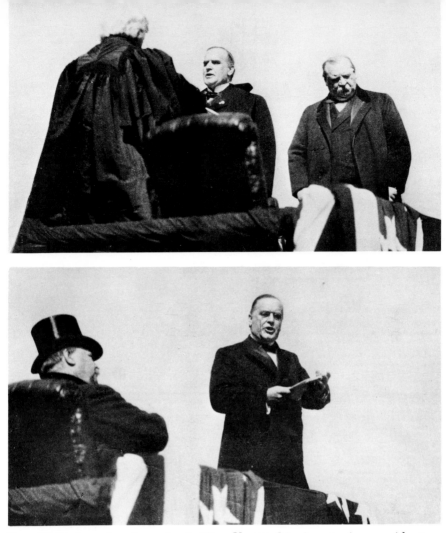

Top: McKinley takes the oath of office. Next to him is outgoing president Grover Cleveland.   Bottom: McKinley delivers his inaugural address.

until every agency of peace has failed." He wished the country to thrive, but not at the expense of human life.

The McKinleys settled into the White House and the president started his new schedule. Every day he answered mail and dealt with the job hunters who tramped into his office. He greeted scores of visitors with his warm smile and his quick, light handshake. On Tuesdays and Fridays, members of the cabinet filed into the White House to discuss government business with the president.

McKinley always carefully measured public opinion before taking political stands. Congressman Joe Cannon once complained, "McKinley keeps his ear to the ground so close that he gets it full of grasshoppers much of the time." Most congressmen, however, marveled at McKinley's kindness and sensitivity. One day, for example, he refused Colorado senator Edward O. Wolcott a political favor but insisted he stay for lunch. "The President was such a gracious host," admitted Wolcott, and I enjoyed myself so much at his table, I almost forgot I had been turned down." Repeatedly McKinley's charm won congressmen over to his views. "We have never had a President who had more influence with Congress than Mr. McKinley," stated Illinois senator Shelby Cullom. McKinley's friendly relationship with Congress allowed him to push for an even higher protective tariff. In 1897 he gladly signed the new Dingley Tariff Act into law.

As always, McKinley paid the greatest personal attention to his ailing wife. Often he slipped away from work to visit her. At official White House dinners it was a tradition that the president escort the wife of the secretary of state. But McKinley abandoned this rule and insisted on sitting next to Ida. More than once the First Lady suffered seizures at these public functions. To limit embarrassment, McKinley would drop his handkerchief over her head until the spasm ended. When Mrs. McKinley recovered, they both would resume their conversations as if nothing unusual had happened. McKinley's obvious love for his wife became admired throughout the capital. Mark Hanna, serving now as an Ohio senator, soon remarked,

A cartoon on the U.S. annexation of Hawaii

"President McKinley has made it pretty hard for the rest of us husbands here in Washington."

As he entered the second year of his term, foreign affairs occupied more of McKinley's time. Americans applauded when he agreed to annex the Hawaiian Islands peacefully. By a joint congressional resolution, those far-off Pacific islands became U.S. territory in July 1898.

Much closer to home, Americans keenly followed activities on the island of Cuba. Since the days of Christopher Columbus Spain had occupied that tropical island, located just ninety miles south of Florida. Tired of Spanish rule, however, in 1895 the Cuban people rose up in open revolt.

With rifles and sharp machetes, Cuban rebels called *insurrectos* attacked Spanish army outposts. Charging out of the jungles, Cuban raiders burned villages, destroyed sugar plantations, and wrecked railroad depots. The Spanish army responded with brutal violence. Soldiers made mass arrests, tortured citizens, and executed suspected rebels. Yelling *"Cuba Libre!"* ("Free Cuba!"), many Americans showed which side they favored in this struggle.

Two rival New York City newspapers took quick advantage of American interest in the Cuban war. The *New York Journal*, owned by William Randolph Hearst, and the *New York World*, owned by Joseph Pulitzer, were in stiff competition for readership. To attract attention, both newspapers used giant banner headlines, favored bold, front-page illustrations, and printed sensational news stories. Both papers published a popular cartoon called "The Yellow Kid," and soon their gaudy style of reporting became known as "yellow journalism."

As Americans clamored for Cuban news, the yellow press rushed correspondents to the island. "You furnish the pictures and I'll furnish the war," publisher Hearst bluntly told one artist he sent. Soon the newsmen were wiring home spectacular reports about the fighting. One article printed in the *World* described Cuba as a place with "blood on the roadsides, blood in the fields, blood on the doorsteps, blood, blood, blood!" Whether true or false, across the United States people snapped up newspapers to read wild stories of gallant *insurrectos*, cruel Spaniards, and bloody violence.

A New York newspaper urges U.S. intervention in Cuba.

For a full year McKinley urged the Spanish to reach a peaceful settlement with the Cubans. Many Americans, he realized, were hungry for war, glory, and new territory. These aggressive patriots, called "jingoes," hoped the United States would be drawn into the Cuban conflict. But McKinley stoutly resisted their pressures. "I have been through one war," he sadly remembered. "I have seen the dead piled up, and I do not want to see another."

In time, though, relations between the United States and Spain grew more strained. In January 1898 Spanish soldiers rioted in Havana, Cuba. The U.S. consul in Havana worried about the safety of Americans living there. Hoping to ease tensions, McKinley ordered the U.S. battleship *Maine* to make a "goodwill" visit.

On February 9, 1898, the *New York Journal* whipped into further excitement. The newspaper obtained and reprinted an insulting personal letter written by Enrique Dupuy de Lome, Spanish ambassador to the United States. In it, de Lome remarked that "McKinley is weak and a bidder for the admiration of the crowd . . . a would-be politician. . . ." In embarrassment, de Lome immediately resigned as ambassador and returned home, but the damage already was done.

A week later total disaster struck in Havana. Since January the battleship *Maine* had rested peacefully moored in Havana harbor. Then on the evening of February 15, 1898, a sudden roaring explosion jolted the *Maine* half out of the water. The fiery blast hurled metal fragments of the warship high into the air. Burned and bloodied sailors shrieked in agony as water rushed into the sinking hull. Of the crew of 354 men, 266 had been killed or drowned. Awakened from his sleep, President McKinley was completely stunned by the news. "The *Maine* blown up! The *Maine* blown up!" he sadly muttered.

Angry Americans blamed the mysterious explosion on the Spanish. "THE WARSHIP MAINE WAS SPLIT IN TWO BY AN ENEMY'S INFERNAL MACHINE," screamed the *New York Journal*. It claimed Spanish spies

A cartoon urging the United States to war

had planted a bomb on the *Maine*. "WAR NOW!" raged
the *World*, calling for immediate revenge. In cities and
towns across the nation people fiercely chanted the slogan:
"Remember the *Maine!* To hell with Spain!"

McKinley still hoped for a peaceful solution to the crisis
and nobly resisted public pressure. "My duty is plain," he
exclaimed. "The Administration . . . will not be plunged
into war until it is ready for it." Most Americans, though,
were itching for a fight. Theodore Roosevelt, the brash
U.S. Assistant Secretary of the Navy, complained that
McKinley had "no more backbone than a chocolate eclair."
"We will have this war for the freedom of Cuba," he
insisted, "in spite of . . . timidity." Other jingoes loudly
echoed Roosevelt's thoughts.

McKinley ordered a U.S. Navy commission to investigate the *Maine* sinking. Its report was unable to fix the responsibility for the tragedy on Spain. Americans, however, bitterly formed their own opinions.

"DESTRUCTION OF THE MAINE BY FOUL PLAY," stormed the *New York World*, adding, ". . . we must punish Spain." After many sleepless nights McKinley caved in at last to the public outcry. On April 11 he asked Congress to grant him war powers. Amid patriotic songs and cheering, on April 25, 1898, Congress declared war against Spain.

Having made his decision, the president quickly called for 125,000 army volunteers. The *New York Sun* happily declared, "We are all jingoes now; and the head jingo is the Hon. William McKinley." While the War Department scrambled to collect guns, ammunition, food, and uniforms for its inexperienced army, a U.S. naval squadron under Commodore George Dewey steamed into immediate action. The Philippine Islands in the Pacific belonged to Spain. On the morning of May 1, 1898, Dewey's cruisers sped forward and attacked the Spanish fleet anchored in Manila Bay.

"You may fire when ready, Gridley," Dewey calmly ordered the captain of his flagship *Olympia*. The great guns of Dewey's squadron and those of the Spanish fleet boomed and belched flame at each other. When the smoke cleared, all of the Spanish ships were destroyed, driven aground, burning, or sinking. The Spaniards lost 381 men killed or injured, while only eight U.S. sailors needed bandaging for slight wounds.

Dewey posing with the *Olympia*'s first gun to fire in the Spanish-American War

When news of this incredible victory reached the United States, Americans wildly waved flags and danced in the streets. Dewey was quickly promoted to admiral and the public made him the hero of the day. Dewey dolls, Dewey toys, Dewey hats, and Dewey buttons instantly appeared for sale. One candy company even invented a gum called "Dewey's Chewies."

The ships of Spain's remaining fleet sailed at top speed across the Atlantic in an effort to protect Cuba. Warships of American commodore Winfield Scott Schley's Atlantic squadron discovered the Spanish fleet at Santiago, Cuba. Quickly the U.S. ships formed a blockade and trapped the enemy vessels inside the harbor.

At Tampa, Florida, the U.S. Fifth Army hurriedly gathered. Many soldiers worried the war would be over before they got a chance to fight. With great confusion the poorly trained volunteers loaded supplies and piled onto cramped transport ships. Finally on June 8 the convoy of 17,000 men commanded by General William Shafter steamed ahead toward Cuba.

President McKinley followed the progress of the war anxiously and carefully. He transformed one White House room into his "War Room." Large maps covered the walls, telegraph wires clicked messages, and assistants answered fifteen telephones. Day and night McKinley signed military commissions, studied dispatches, and discussed strategy. George Cortelyou, McKinley's private secretary, one day noted in his diary, "The President is again looking careworn, the color having faded from his cheeks. . . . The strain upon him is terrible."

By the end of June 1898 good news relieved McKinley a little. General Shafter's army had landed on the southern coast of Cuba. Marching inland through the sweltering jungle, these troops soon reached the outskirts of Santiago. Blocking the way to the north stood the fortified village of El Caney. To the west rose the San Juan Heights, defended by barbed wire, trenches, and blockhouses. On the morning of July 1 Shafter ordered these positions attacked.

Cannon roared and rapid-fire Gatling guns swept bullets through El Caney's streets. Sweating in their heavy blue flannel shirts and khaki trousers, the U.S. soldiers charged bravely into the town. Within a few hours the American flag waved above El Caney.

The capture of Santiago

At the foot of the San Juan Heights (which included San Juan Hill and Kettle Hill), troopers impatiently waited for their final orders. One officer was Colonel Theodore Roosevelt. At the start of the war Roosevelt had quit his government position and had formed a special volunteer cavalry regiment. Filled with lean cowboys, sharpshooting Indians, and Ivy League college athletes, the outfit came to be known as "Roosevelt's Rough Riders."

Theodore Roosevelt and his Rough Riders

When Roosevelt at last received word to advance, he galloped along the battle line. "Follow me!" he yelled. Eager Rough Riders mixed together with white and black troopers from other U.S. regiments. "I waved my hat," Roosevelt later exclaimed, "and we went up the hill in a rush." With Roosevelt in the lead, the soldiers swarmed up Kettle Hill. The frightened Spaniards threw down their guns and scampered in retreat. Before the day was through, the American troops had conquered all of the San Juan Heights. In the distance they gazed at the rooftops of Santiago. News of Roosevelt's valiant charge electrified the United States. Overnight the event made him even more famous than Admiral Dewey.

Nearly surrounded now, Admiral Pascual Cervera desperately tried to save his Spanish fleet. On the morning of July 3, 1898, Cervera's four Spanish cruisers and two torpedo boats steamed out of Santiago harbor. Aboard the U.S. blockade ship *Brooklyn*, Commodore Schley quickly raised signal flags: "Clear all ships for action. Engage the enemy." The huge guns of the U.S. battleships sent shells shrieking through the sky. Within hours the naval battle of Santiago ended. Unable to escape, all of the Spanish ships soon were sunken, beached, or burning.

In the United States, people greeted this latest news with screeching train whistles, clanging church bells, and banging gun salutes. No one could have been happier than President McKinley.

The loss of these last Spanish ships spelled the doom of Santiago and all of Cuba. Soon after, another U.S. Army expedition easily captured the neighboring Spanish island of Puerto Rico. In complete defeat, Spain asked for a cease-fire and peace negotiations. On August 12, 1898, Spain agreed to Cuban independence and gave up Puerto Rico to the United States. The fate of the Philippines would be decided later at a Paris peace conference.

After only 110 days of fighting the Spanish-American War was over. Fifteen hundred U.S. soldiers had been killed or wounded. Hundreds more had fallen victim to tropical diseases such as malaria and yellow fever. Still, Americans wildly celebrated their victory. "It's been a splendid little war," declared American diplomat John Hay. Only a few people argued that it was a totally needless war, provoked by the yellow press, and won by luck.

Chapter 6

Joining the Great
World Powers

Through the autumn months McKinley turned his attention to the future of the Philippines. "If Old Dewey had just sailed away when he smashed that Spanish fleet," he remarked, "what a lot of trouble he would have saved us." Some people claimed the Filipino natives could govern themselves and deserved their independence. Others believed the United States should not entangle itself in foreign affairs. Most Americans, however, looked upon the Philippines as conquered territory fairly won. They demanded the United States keep the islands.

Unable to decide, McKinley admitted, "I walked the floor of the White House night after night." Only after weighing every scrap of information, gathering advice, and listening to public opinion did he reach his conclusion. "Isolation is no longer possible or desirable," he declared. "A high and sacred obligation rests upon the Government of the United States to give protection . . . and wise, firm and unselfish guidance . . . to all the people of the Philippine Islands."

Opposite page: Western powers try to
impose an "open door" policy on China.

Meeting at the Paris peace talks, U.S. commissioners demanded that Spain give up the Philippines in exchange for twenty million dollars. The Spaniards also surrendered the little Pacific island of Guam. On December 10, 1898, the formal Treaty of Paris was signed.

Thrilled American jingoes quickly examined maps to learn where the new territories were located. The Philippine Islands were of strategic military importance and offered new markets for U.S. products.

Filipino revolutionaries led by Emilio Aquinaldo resented their new American rulers as much as they had the Spanish. During the next two years, U.S. troops battled Filipino guerrillas in bloody jungle skirmishes. The fighting only ended with the capture of Aquinaldo in March 1901. Three months later McKinley established a peaceful civil government in the Philippines, and future U.S. president William Howard Taft took the oath as its first colonial governor. The Philippine Islands remained U.S. territory until independence was granted in 1946.

As the United States entered the 1900s, McKinley showed his growing interest in international affairs. China possessed a weak government, and several foreign countries tried to monopolize China's rich trade opportunities. The United States wished to develop Chinese markets, too. In 1898 McKinley proposed his "Open Door" policy. "Asking only the open door for ourselves," he addressed the great world powers, "we are ready to accord the open door to others." Peacefully America joined Britain, France, Germany, Russia, and Japan on an equal footing in the China trade.

U.S. Marines battling the Boxers in Peking in 1900

Certain Chinese nationalists hated the presence of the foreigners in their country. One secret society was nicknamed the Boxers because of their ritual fighting exercises. In June 1900 the Boxers openly rebelled against foreign influences. Rioters hacked Western missionaries to death and attacked the foreign community in the city of Peking. Sympathetic Chinese troops did little to stop the wild mobs. American diplomats and businessmen barricaded themselves inside the British Legation compound with other frightened foreigners. One American official anxiously wrote, "We are besieged in Peking, entirely cut off from outside communications and our deliverance depends on . . . concerted action . . . coming to our relief."

U.S. troops on guard at the American consulate in Peking

Immediately McKinley ordered five thousand U.S. troops to join an international relief expedition with seven other nations. In August 1900 this foreign army marched inland from the Chinese coast. Swiftly they broke the Peking siege and ended the Boxer Rebellion. For the time being, China's "Open Door" would remain open.

Four years of heavy responsibilities left McKinley feeling exhausted. When the Republican national convention opened in June of 1900, however, the hugely popular president seemed the overwhelming choice of delegates. One June 19 bands blared "Rally 'Round the Flag" and "There'll Be a Hot Time in the Old Town Tonight." Adding to the noise, delegates yelled themselves hoarse and unanimously voted to nominate McKinley again.

No one questioned that McKinley would be their choice. Many delegates wondered, though, whom to pick for the vice-presidential candidate. Vice-President Hobart had died in office in November 1899. As delegates pondered lists of possibilities, McKinley issued a statement from the White House. "The President has no choice for Vice-President. Any of the distinguished names suggested would be satisfactory to him. The choice of the convention will be his choice. . . . "

After the Spanish-American War, New Yorkers had elected Theodore Roosevelt governor. In less than a year, Roosevelt's vigorous reform policies upset old-guard New York Republicans. Now they saw a chance to push him out of New York by making him vice-president.

On the convention floor, New York delegates shouted Roosevelt's name; hundreds of others jumped onto their chairs and joined the yell. Roosevelt, the heroic Rough Rider, captured their imaginations. Souvenir hawkers quickly sold all of their "McKinley-Roosevelt" buttons and badges. New York senator Thomas Platt happily observed, "Roosevelt might as well stand under Niagara Falls and try to spit water back as to stop his nomination by this convention." Republican chairman Mark Hanna, however, feared Roosevelt's reputation for wildness.

"Don't any of you realize," he complained, "there's only one life between this madman and the White House?"

In the end, by a vote of 925 to 1, the convention nominated Roosevelt to run with McKinley. Only Delegate Roosevelt modestly refused to vote for himself.

LIFE'S FASHIONS FOR 1900.

MORNING SUIT FOR GENTLEMAN OF MEANS, AND FOR BUTTONS.

McKinley (right) is shown as a servant to wealthy Mark Hanna.

The Democrats picked William Jennings Bryan to be their national candidate again. Through the summer and fall Bryan once more stumped across the country. He claimed the U.S. gold standard remained unfair to farmers. McKinley's policies, he insisted, represented the interests of the rich. He also attacked the president's "imperialist" actions in the Philippines. Bryan wished to see the islands granted their full independence.

McKinley did not campaign openly and only delivered a few front-porch speeches. Theodore Roosevelt, however, stampeded 21,000 miles, crisscrossing the country in support of the Republican ticket. Mark Hanna's political organization also handed out tons of McKinley literature, and faithful Republicans yelled the slogan: "Four Years More of the Full Dinner Pail."

Campaign poster for McKinley and Roosevelt

On election eve that November, Canton townspeople paraded to McKinley's house. Drums banged and horns blew and people cheered until the Major stepped out to say a few thankful words. Everyone seemed certain of a Republican triumph at the polls the next day.

After Americans voted and officials tallied up the ballots on November 6, banner newspaper headlines finally reported:

	Popular Vote	Electoral Vote
William McKinley	7,218,039	292
William Jennings Bryan	6,358,345	155

McKinley had beaten his opponent in an impressive landslide. To a friend he soon stated with deep emotion, "I can no longer be called the President of a party; I am now the President of the whole people."

Bernard Partridge.

Chapter 7

Death of a President

Companies of cavalrymen in neatly pressed uniforms rode up Pennsylvania Avenue, and marching clubs proudly trooped past the watching crowds. Though clouds hung heavily overhead on March 4, 1901, they failed to keep visitors from Washington, D.C. People jostled together shoulder-to-shoulder to witness the first presidential inauguration of the twentieth century.

Late in the morning the president's carriage rolled out of the White House drive. Along the route to the Capitol, McKinley smiled at the waving spectators. At noon masses of people watched him step out onto the Capitol's east portico. A drizzle began and umbrellas popped open as it turned into a pelting rain. "This is not McKinley weather," remarked one congressman.

Most people, however, braved the wetness to hear McKinley take his second oath of office and deliver his inaugural address. In ringing tones he asked Americans to help him in fulfilling the nation's destiny. He called for peacefulness and patience in world affairs. Regardless of the soaking rain, the gathering loudly applauded the speech. With McKinley as president, Americans felt sure of the country's continued success.

McKinley's first action in his second term was to take a six-week tour across the nation. On April 29 the festooned presidential train chugged out of the Washington station. At whistle-stops across the South and West, President and Mrs. McKinley greatly enjoyed greeting the public. The strain on the First Lady's fragile health, however, soon proved too great. In San Francisco, California, she fell gravely ill. McKinley stayed by her side until the danger passed and they could return to Canton.

In September McKinley decided to fulfill a promise to attend the great Pan-American Exposition being held in Buffalo, New York. Among the fair's international exhibits were displays that showed American technical advances in electrical machinery, the automobile, and the telephone. McKinley journeyed to Buffalo in a spirit of curiosity and enthusiasm.

A festive mood filled the crowd that flocked to the fairgrounds on September 5. On a specially built platform McKinley addressed a sea of eager faces. In his speech he praised the nation's progress and reminded his listeners that the country's true greatness "rests in the victories of peace, not those of war."

McKinley's schedule for the following day, September 6, included a visit to nearby Niagara Falls. In the afternoon, however, he returned to the Exposition to hold a brief public reception at the Temple of Music. Secret Service agents worried about security at the widely advertised reception. McKinley, however, never imagined anyone would wish to harm him. He expected this to be a restful day and he looked forward to meeting the people.

Last photograph of President McKinley, taken while he was going up the steps of the Temple of Music, Friday, September 6, 1901

At four o'clock, neatly dressed in pin-striped trousers, a dark frock coat, and a black satin cravat, McKinley signaled for the doors of the Temple of Music to be opened. Smiling with eagerness, people stepped forward on the reception line. Others packed the upstairs galleries and watched the president admiringly. No one took special notice of the twenty-eight-year-old man with the handkerchief wrapped around his hand, until suddenly two gunshots shattered the afternoon's sunny, joyful atmosphere. "What is it? What has happened?" stunned witnesses wondered aloud.

Leon Czolgosz shoots President McKinley in the Temple of Music.

Guards scuffled with the man and threw him to the floor. Others rushed to the president's side and helped him to a chair. Panicked shouts and screams soon alerted people that an assassin had shot McKinley.

Within minutes an electric-powered ambulance sped the wounded president to the Exposition's little emergency hospital. Several local doctors pressed close around the operating table. The first bullet had fallen out of the president's clothes. It had only bruised his ribs. The second, though, remained buried deep inside his body. Still conscious, McKinley consented to an immediate operation.

The doctors administered ether to their patient and began the critical surgery. Doctor Matthew D. Mann carefully sliced into McKinley's abdomen, following the path of the hidden bullet. He sewed closed the holes in the president's stomach. But the bullet had passed even deeper, lodging somewhere near his back. Unable to find it in the failing afternoon light, the doctors cleaned the wound as well as possible and sewed it up. Although a new X-ray machine was on display at the Exposition, it was never used to locate the bullet. In the evening the ambulance transferred McKinley to the 1168 Delaware Avenue home of John G. Milburn, the director of the Exposition.

Soon hundreds of people stood outside waiting for hopeful news of the president. They whispered as high government officials hurriedly arrived at the house. Inside, Ida McKinley stayed close by her husband's side during his time of need. During the next two days the president seemed steadily to improve.

McKinley calmly asked to see George Cortelyou. "It's mighty lonesome in here," the president weakly greeted his secretary with a smile. After Vice-President Roosevelt visited the sickroom he stated his belief that McKinley was "coming along splendidly" and "on the high road to recovery." On September 11, doctors allowed him a meal of chicken broth, toast, and coffee, his first solid food.

The next day, however, his temperature began to rise, his mind wandered, and his overall condition rapidly worsened. Deadly gangrene had developed in his wound. On Friday, September 13, bulletins flashed the latest news across the nation: "The President is sinking."

The Temple of Music at Buffalo's Pan-American Exposition

Grief-stricken friends and relatives waited near the dying man's bedside. Late in the afternoon McKinley whispered to his doctors, "It is useless, gentlemen. I think we ought to have a prayer." In the evening his wife sat close beside him. "Good-bye, good-bye all," he weakly breathed. "It is God's way. His will, not ours, be done." Then he repeated words from his favorite hymn, "Nearer My God to Thee." Ida McKinley hugged her husband and wept, "I want to go too. I want to go too."

"We are all going," murmured McKinley, "We are all going."

That night he fell into a coma, and at 2:15 A.M. on September 14, 1901, President McKinley died.

Leon Czolgosz in his prison cell

Rushing back to Buffalo from a camping trip in New York's Adirondack Mountains, Theodore Roosevelt solemnly took the oath of office as twenty-sixth U.S. president. Afterwards he announced, "I wish to say that it shall be my aim to continue, absolutely unbroken, the policy of President McKinley for the peace, the prosperity, and the honor of our beloved country."

When questioned, the insane murderer, Leon Czolgosz, openly admitted, "I killed President McKinley because I done my duty. I don't believe one man should have so much service and another man should have none." At his trial, the jury quickly found him guilty of the ugly deed. In October, at New York's Auburn State Prison, the condemned man was executed in the electric chair.

McKinley's coffin is unloaded from the funeral train.

For many days following President McKinley's death, Americans deeply mourned. Flags fell to half-staff, church bells tolled, and doors were draped with black. Thousands of tearful citizens crowded along the tracks as a train carried the body to Washington. Thousands more viewed the casket in the Capitol rotunda. Then, as a second funeral train bore the coffin to its burial place in Canton, more Americans lined the route and waved their sad farewells.

William McKinley (1843-1901), as president, at his desk in the White House

"All our people loved their dead President," remarked former president Grover Cleveland. "His kindly nature . . . lovable traits of character, and . . . consideration for all about him will long live in the minds and hearts of his countrymen." As the nation moved forward into the twentieth century, it was clear that William McKinley had left his mark. Carefully he had guided the country out of its old-fashioned past, enabling high-spirited Americans to plunge ahead into the modern age.

Above: President McKinley (left) sits with his cabinet during a meeting in the White House. At center (front) is Secretary of State John Hay. Next to him is Secretary of War Elihu Root.

Left: President McKinley in the Government Building of the Pan-American Exposition on September 5, 1901, the day before he was shot

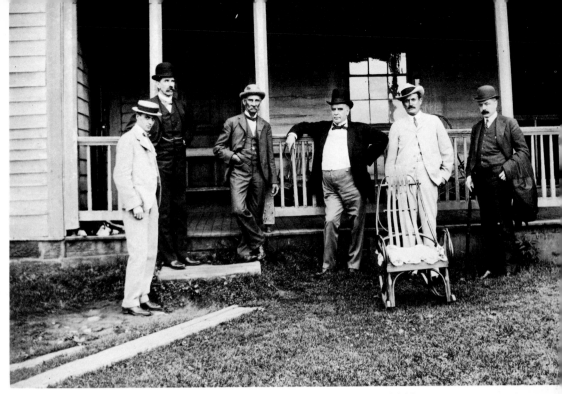

Above: McKinley with some friends at his farm in 1901
Below: The philosophy of the president

Our Destiny

Where our artisans have the admitted capacity to excel, where our inventive genius has initiated many of the grandest discoveries of these later days, and where the native resources of our land are as limitless as they are valuable to supply the world's needs, it is our province, as it should be our earnest care, to lead in the march of human progress, and not rest content with any secondary place.

Chronology of American History

(Shaded area covers events in William McKinley's lifetime.)

About A.D. 982 — Eric the Red, born in Norway, reaches Greenland in one of the first European voyages to North America.

About 1000 — Leif Ericson (Eric the Red's son) leads what is thought to be the first European expedition to mainland North America; Leif probably lands in Canada.

1492 — Christopher Columbus, seeking a sea route from Spain to the Far East, discovers the New World.

1497 — John Cabot reaches Canada in the first English voyage to North America.

1513 — Ponce de Léon explores Florida in search of the fabled Fountain of Youth.

1519-1521 — Hernando Cortés of Spain conquers Mexico.

1534 — French explorers led by Jacques Cartier enter the Gulf of St. Lawrence in Canada.

1540 — Spanish explorer Francisco Coronado begins exploring the American Southwest, seeking the riches of the mythical Seven Cities of Cibola.

1565 — St. Augustine, Florida, the first permanent European town in what is now the United States, is founded by the Spanish.

1607 — Jamestown, Virginia, is founded, the first permanent English town in the present-day U.S.

1608 — Frenchman Samuel de Champlain founds the village of Quebec, Canada.

1609 — Henry Hudson explores the eastern coast of present-day U.S. for the Netherlands; the Dutch then claim parts of New York, New Jersey, Delaware, and Connecticut and name the area New Netherland.

1619 — The English colonies' first shipment of black slaves arrives in Jamestown.

1620 — English Pilgrims found Massachusetts' first permanent town at Plymouth.

1621 — Massachusetts Pilgrims and Indians hold the famous first Thanksgiving feast in colonial America.

1623 — Colonization of New Hampshire is begun by the English.

1624 — Colonization of present-day New York State is begun by the Dutch at Fort Orange (Albany).

1625 — The Dutch start building New Amsterdam (now New York City).

1630 — The town of Boston, Massachusetts, is founded by the English Puritans.

1633 — Colonization of Connecticut is begun by the English.

1634 — Colonization of Maryland is begun by the English.

1636 — Harvard, the colonies' first college, is founded in Massachusetts. Rhode Island colonization begins when Englishman Roger Williams founds Providence.

1638 — Delaware colonization begins as Swedes build Fort Christina at present-day Wilmington.

1640 — Stephen Daye of Cambridge, Massachusetts prints *The Bay Psalm Book*, the first English-language book published in what is now the U.S.

1643 — Swedish settlers begin colonizing Pennsylvania.

About 1650 — North Carolina is colonized by Virginia settlers.

1660 — New Jersey colonization is begun by the Dutch at present-day Jersey City.

1670 — South Carolina colonization is begun by the English near Charleston.

1673 — Jacques Marquette and Louis Jolliet explore the upper Mississippi River for France.

1682—Philadelphia, Pennsylvania, is settled. La Salle explores Mississippi River all the way to its mouth in Louisiana and claims the whole Mississippi Valley for France.

1693—College of William and Mary is founded in Williamsburg, Virginia.

1700—Colonial population is about 250,000.

1703—Benjamin Franklin is born in Boston.

1732—George Washington, first president of the U.S., is born in Westmoreland County, Virginia.

1733—James Oglethorpe founds Savannah, Georgia; Georgia is established as the thirteenth colony.

1735—John Adams, second president of the U.S., is born in Braintree, Massachusetts.

1737—William Byrd founds Richmond, Virginia.

1738—British troops are sent to Georgia over border dispute with Spain.

1739—Black insurrection takes place in South Carolina.

1740—English Parliament passes act allowing naturalization of immigrants to American colonies after seven-year residence.

1743—Thomas Jefferson is born in Albemarle County, Virginia. Benjamin Franklin retires at age thirty-seven to devote himself to scientific inquiries and public service.

1744—King George's War begins; France joins war effort against England.

1745—During King George's War, France raids settlements in Maine and New York.

1747—Classes begin at Princeton College in New Jersey.

1748—The Treaty of Aix-la-Chapelle concludes King George's War.

1749—Parliament legally recognizes slavery in colonies and the inauguration of the plantation system in the South. George Washington becomes the surveyor for Culpepper County in Virginia.

1750—Thomas Walker passes through and names Cumberland Gap on his way toward Kentucky region. Colonial population is about 1,200,000.

1751—James Madison, fourth president of the U.S., is born in Port Conway, Virginia. English Parliament passes Currency Act, banning New England colonies from issuing paper money. George Washington travels to Barbados.

1752—Pennsylvania Hospital, the first general hospital in the colonies, is founded in Philadelphia. Benjamin Franklin uses a kite in a thunderstorm to demonstrate that lightning is a form of electricity.

1753—George Washington delivers command that the French withdraw from the Ohio River Valley; French disregard the demand. Colonial population is about 1,328,000.

1754—French and Indian War begins (extends to Europe as the Seven Years' War). Washington surrenders at Fort Necessity.

1755—French and Indians ambush Braddock. Washington becomes commander of Virginia troops.

1756—England declares war on France.

1758—James Monroe, fifth president of the U.S., is born in Westmoreland County, Virginia.

1759—Cherokee Indian war begins in southern colonies; hostilities extend to 1761. George Washington marries Martha Dandridge Custis.

1760—George III becomes king of England. Colonial population is about 1,600,000.

1762—England declares war on Spain.

1763—Treaty of Paris concludes the French and Indian War and the Seven Years' War. England gains Canada and most other French lands east of the Mississippi River.

1764—British pass the Sugar Act to gain tax money from the colonists. The issue of taxation without representation is first introduced in Boston. John Adams marries Abigail Smith.

1765—Stamp Act goes into effect in the colonies. Business virtually stops as almost all colonists refuse to use the stamps.

1766—British repeal the Stamp Act.

1767—John Quincy Adams, sixth president of the U.S. and son of second president John Adams, is born in Braintree, Massachusetts. Andrew Jackson, seventh president of the U.S., is born in Waxhaw settlement, South Carolina.

1769—Daniel Boone sights the Kentucky Territory.

1770—In the Boston Massacre, British soldiers kill five colonists and injure six. Townshend Acts are repealed, thus eliminating all duties on imports to the colonies except tea.

1771—Benjamin Franklin begins his autobiography, a work that he will never complete. The North Carolina assembly passes the "Bloody Act," which makes rioters guilty of treason.

1772—Samuel Adams rouses colonists to consider British threats to self-government.

1773—English Parliament passes the Tea Act. Colonists dressed as Mohawk Indians board British tea ships and toss 342 casks of tea into the water in what becomes known as the Boston Tea Party. William Henry Harrison is born in Charles City County, Virginia.

1774—British close the port of Boston to punish the city for the Boston Tea Party. First Continental Congress convenes in Philadelphia.

1775—American Revolution begins with battles of Lexington and Concord, Massachusetts. Second Continental Congress opens in Philadelphia. George Washington becomes commander-in-chief of the Continental army.

1776—Declaration of Independence is adopted on July 4.

1777—Congress adopts the American flag with thirteen stars and thirteen stripes. John Adams is sent to France to negotiate peace treaty.

1778—France declares war against Great Britain and becomes U.S. ally.

1779—British surrender to Americans at Vincennes. Thomas Jefferson is elected governor of Virginia. James Madison is elected to the Continental Congress.

1780—Benedict Arnold, first American traitor, defects to the British.

1781—Articles of Confederation go into effect. Cornwallis surrenders to George Washington at Yorktown, ending the American Revolution.

1782—American commissioners, including John Adams, sign peace treaty with British in Paris. Thomas Jefferson's wife, Martha, dies. Martin Van Buren is born in Kinderhook, New York.

1784—Zachary Taylor is born near Barboursville, Virginia.

1785—Congress adopts the dollar as the unit of currency. John Adams is made minister to Great Britain. Thomas Jefferson is appointed minister to France.

1786—Shays's Rebellion begins in Massachusetts.

1787—Constitutional Convention assembles in Philadelphia, with George Washington presiding; U.S. Constitution is adopted. Delaware, New Jersey, and Pennsylvania become states.

1788—Virginia, South Carolina, New York, Connecticut, New Hampshire, Maryland, and Massachusetts become states. U.S. Constitution is ratified. New York City is declared U.S. capital.

1789—Presidential electors elect George Washington and John Adams as first president and vice-president. Thomas Jefferson is appointed secretary of state. North Carolina becomes a state. French Revolution begins.

1790—Supreme Court meets for the first time. Rhode Island becomes a state. First national census in the U.S. counts 3,929,214 persons. John Tyler is born in Charles City County, Virginia.

1791—Vermont enters the Union. U.S. Bill of Rights, the first ten amendments to the Constitution, goes into effect. District of Columbia is established. James Buchanan is born in Stony Batter, Pennsylvania.

1792—Thomas Paine publishes *The Rights of Man*. Kentucky becomes a state. Two political parties are formed in the U.S., Federalist and Republican. Washington is elected to a second term, with Adams as vice-president.

1793—War between France and Britain begins; U.S. declares neutrality. Eli Whitney invents the cotton gin; cotton production and slave labor increase in the South.

1794—Eleventh Amendment to the Constitution is passed, limiting federal courts' power. "Whiskey Rebellion" in Pennsylvania protests federal whiskey tax. James Madison marries Dolley Payne Todd.

1795—George Washington signs the Jay Treaty with Great Britain. Treaty of San Lorenzo, between U.S. and Spain, settles Florida boundary and gives U.S. right to navigate the Mississippi. James Polk is born near Pineville, North Carolina.

1796—Tennessee enters the Union. Washington gives his Farewell Address, refusing a third presidential term. John Adams is elected president and Thomas Jefferson vice-president.

1797—Adams recommends defense measures against possible war with France. Napoleon Bonaparte and his army march against Austrians in Italy. U.S. population is about 4,900,000.

1798—Washington is named commander-in-chief of the U.S. Army. Department of the Navy is created. Alien and Sedition Acts are passed. Napoleon's troops invade Egypt and Switzerland.

1799—George Washington dies at Mount Vernon, New York. James Monroe is elected governor of Virginia. French Revolution ends. Napoleon becomes ruler of France.

1800—Thomas Jefferson and Aaron Burr tie for president. U.S. capital is moved from Philadelphia to Washington, D.C. The White House is built as presidents' home. Spain returns Louisiana to France. Millard Fillmore is born in Locke, New York.

1801—After thirty-six ballots, House of Representatives elects Thomas Jefferson president, making Burr vice-president. James Madison is named secretary of state.

1802—Congress abolishes excise taxes. U.S. Military Academy is founded at West Point, New York.

1803—Ohio enters the Union. Louisiana Purchase treaty is signed with France, greatly expanding U.S. territory.

1804—Twelfth Amendment to the Constitution rules that president and vice-president be elected separately. Alexander Hamilton is killed by Vice-President Aaron Burr in a duel. Orleans Territory is established. Napoleon crowns himself emperor of France. Franklin Pierce is born in Hillsborough Lower Village, New Hampshire.

1805—Thomas Jefferson begins his second term as president. Lewis and Clark expedition reaches the Pacific Ocean.

1806—Coinage of silver dollars is stopped; resumes in 1836.

1807—Aaron Burr is acquitted in treason trial. Embargo Act closes U.S. ports to trade.

1808—James Madison is elected president. Congress outlaws importing slaves from Africa. Andrew Johnson is born in Raleigh, North Carolina.

1809—Abraham Lincoln is born near Hodgenville, Kentucky.

1810—U.S. population is 7,240,000.

1811—William Henry Harrison defeats Indians at Tippecanoe. Monroe is named secretary of state.

1812—Louisiana becomes a state. U.S. declares war on Britain (War of 1812). James Madison is reelected president. Napoleon invades Russia.

1813—British forces take Fort Niagara and Buffalo, New York.

1814—Francis Scott Key writes "The Star-Spangled Banner." British troops burn much of Washington, D.C., including the White House. Treaty of Ghent ends War of 1812. James Monroe becomes secretary of war.

1815—Napoleon meets his final defeat at Battle of Waterloo.

1816—James Monroe is elected president. Indiana becomes a state.

1817—Mississippi becomes state. Construction on Erie Canal begins.

1818—Illinois enters the Union. The present thirteen-stripe flag is adopted. Border between U.S. and Canada is agreed upon.

1819—Alabama becomes a state. U.S. purchases Florida from Spain. Thomas Jefferson establishes the University of Virginia.

1820—James Monroe is reelected. In the Missouri Compromise, Maine enters the Union as a free (non-slave) state.

1821—Missouri enters the Union as a slave state. Santa Fe Trail opens the American Southwest. Mexico declares independence from Spain. Napoleon Bonaparte dies.

1822—U.S. recognizes Mexico and Colombia. Liberia in Africa is founded as a home for freed slaves. Ulysses S. Grant is born in Point Pleasant, Ohio. Rutherford B. Hayes is born in Delaware, Ohio.

1823—Monroe Doctrine closes North and South America to European colonizing or invasion.

1824—House of Representatives elects John Quincy Adams president when none of the four candidates wins a majority in national election. Mexico becomes a republic.

1825—Erie Canal is opened. U.S. population is 11,300,000.

1826—Thomas Jefferson and John Adams both die on July 4, the fiftieth anniversary of the Declaration of Independence.

1828—Andrew Jackson is elected president. Tariff of Abominations is passed, cutting imports.

1829—James Madison attends Virginia's constitutional convention. Slavery is abolished in Mexico. Chester A. Arthur is born in Fairfield, Vermont.

1830—Indian Removal Act to resettle Indians west of the Mississippi is approved.

1831—James Monroe dies in New York City. James A. Garfield is born in Orange, Ohio. Cyrus McCormick develops his reaper.

1832—Andrew Jackson, nominated by the new Democratic Party, is reelected president.

1833—Britain abolishes slavery in its colonies. Benjamin Harrison is born in North Bend, Ohio.

1835—Federal government becomes debt-free for the first time.

1836—Martin Van Buren becomes president. Texas wins independence from Mexico. Arkansas joins the Union. James Madison dies at Montpelier, Virginia.

1837—Michigan enters the Union. U.S. population is 15,900,000. Grover Cleveland is born in Caldwell, New Jersey.

1840—William Henry Harrison is elected president.

1841—President Harrison dies in Washington, D.C., one month after inauguration. Vice-President John Tyler succeeds him.

1843—William McKinley is born in Niles, Ohio.

1844—James Knox Polk is elected president. Samuel Morse sends first telegraphic message.

1845—Texas and Florida become states. Potato famine in Ireland causes massive emigration from Ireland to U.S. Andrew Jackson dies near Nashville, Tennessee.

1846—Iowa enters the Union. War with Mexico begins.

1847—U.S. captures Mexico City.

1848—Zachary Taylor becomes president. Treaty of Guadalupe Hidalgo ends Mexico-U.S. war. Wisconsin becomes a state.

1849—James Polk dies in Nashville, Tennessee.

1850—President Taylor dies in Washington, D.C.; Vice-President Millard Fillmore succeeds him. California enters the Union, breaking tie between slave and free states.

1852—Franklin Pierce is elected president.

1853—Gadsden Purchase transfers Mexican territory to U.S.

1854—"War for Bleeding Kansas" is fought between slave and free states.

1855—Czar Nicholas I of Russia dies, succeeded by Alexander II.

1856—James Buchanan is elected president. In Massacre of Potawatomi Creek, Kansas-slavers are murdered by free-staters. Woodrow Wilson is born in Staunton, Pennsylvania.

1857—William Howard Taft is born in Cincinnati, Ohio.

1858—Minnesota enters the Union. Theodore Roosevelt is born in New York City.

1859—Oregon becomes a state.

1860—Abraham Lincoln is elected president; South Carolina secedes from the Union in protest.

1861—Arkansas, Tennessee, North Carolina, and Virginia secede. Kansas enters the Union as a free state. Civil War begins.

1862—Union forces capture Fort Henry, Roanoke Island, Fort Donelson, Jacksonville, and New Orleans; Union armies are defeated at the battles of Bull Run and Fredericksburg. Martin Van Buren dies in Kinderhook, New York. John Tyler dies near Charles City, Virginia.

1863—Lincoln issues Emancipation Proclamation: all slaves held in rebelling territories are declared free. West Virginia becomes a state.

1864—Abraham Lincoln is reelected. Nevada becomes a state.

1865—Lincoln is assassinated in Washington, D.C., and succeeded by Andrew Johnson. U.S. Civil War ends on May 26. Thirteenth Amendment abolishes slavery. Warren G. Harding is born in Blooming Grove, Ohio.

1867—Nebraska becomes a state. U.S. buys Alaska from Russia for $7,200,000. Reconstruction Acts are passed.

1868—President Johnson is impeached for violating Tenure of Office Act, but is acquitted by Senate. Ulysses S. Grant is elected president. Fourteenth Amendment prohibits voting discrimination. James Buchanan dies in Lancaster, Pennsylvania.

1869—Franklin Pierce dies in Concord, New Hampshire.

1870—Fifteenth Amendment gives blacks the right to vote.

1872—Grant is reelected over Horace Greeley. General Amnesty Act pardons ex-Confederates. Calvin Coolidge is born in Plymouth Notch, Vermont.

1874—Millard Fillmore dies in Buffalo, New York. Herbert Hoover is born in West Branch, Iowa.

1875—Andrew Johnson dies in Carter's Station, Tennessee.

1876—Colorado enters the Union. "Custer's last stand": he and his men are massacred by Sioux Indians at Little Big Horn, Montana.

1877—Rutherford B. Hayes is elected president as all disputed votes are awarded to him.

1880—James A. Garfield is elected president.

1881—President Garfield is assassinated and dies in Elberon, New Jersey. Vice-President Chester A. Arthur succeeds him.

1882—U.S. bans Chinese immigration. Franklin D. Roosevelt is born in Hyde Park, New York.

1885—Ulysses S. Grant dies in Mount McGregor, New York.

1886—Statue of Liberty is dedicated. Chester A. Arthur dies in New York City.

1888—Benjamin Harrison is elected president.

1889—North Dakota, South Dakota, Washington, and Montana become states.

1890—Dwight D. Eisenhower is born in Denison, Texas. Idaho and Wyoming become states.

1892—Grover Cleveland is elected president.

1893—Rutherford B. Hayes dies in Fremont, Ohio.

1896—William McKinley is elected president. Utah becomes a state.

1898—U.S. declares war on Spain over Cuba.

1899—Philippines demand independence from U.S.

1900—McKinley is reelected. Boxer Rebellion against foreigners in China begins.

1901—McKinley is assassinated by anarchist Leon Czolgosz in Buffalo, New York; Theodore Roosevelt becomes president. Benjamin Harrison dies in Indianapolis, Indiana.

1902—U.S. acquires perpetual control over Panama Canal.

1903—Alaskan frontier is settled.

1904—Russian-Japanese War breaks out. Theodore Roosevelt wins presidential election.

1905—Treaty of Portsmouth signed, ending Russian-Japanese War.

1906—U.S. troops occupy Cuba.

1907—President Roosevelt bars all Japanese immigration. Oklahoma enters the Union.

1908—William Howard Taft becomes president. Grover Cleveland dies in Princeton, New Jersey. Lyndon B. Johnson is born near Stonewall, Texas.

1909—NAACP is founded under W.E.B. DuBois

1910—China abolishes slavery.

1911—Chinese Revolution begins. Ronald Reagan is born in Tampico, Illinois.

1912—Woodrow Wilson is elected president. Arizona and New Mexico become states.

1913—Federal income tax is introduced in U.S. through the Sixteenth Amendment. Richard Nixon is born in Yorba Linda, California. Gerald Ford is born in Omaha, Nebraska.

1914—World War I begins.

1915—British liner *Lusitania* is sunk by German submarine.

1916—Wilson is reelected president.

1917—U.S. breaks diplomatic relations with Germany. Czar Nicholas of Russia abdicates as revolution begins. U.S. declares war on Austria-Hungary. John F. Kennedy is born in Brookline, Massachusetts.

1918—Wilson proclaims "Fourteen Points" as war aims. On November 11, armistice is signed between Allies and Germany.

1919—Eighteenth Amendment prohibits sale and manufacture of intoxicating liquors. Wilson presides over first League of Nations; wins Nobel Peace Prize. Theodore Roosevelt dies in Oyster Bay, New York.

1920—Nineteenth Amendment (women's suffrage) is passed. Warren Harding is elected president.

1921—Adolf Hitler's stormtroopers begin to terrorize political opponents.

1922—Irish Free State is established. Soviet states form USSR. Benito Mussolini forms Fascist government in Italy.

1923—President Harding dies in San Francisco, California; he is succeeded by Vice-President Calvin Coolidge.

1924—Coolidge is elected president. Woodrow Wilson dies in Washington, D.C. James Carter is born in Plains, Georgia.

1925—Hitler reorganizes Nazi Party and publishes first volume of *Mein Kampf*.

1926—Fascist youth organizations founded in Germany and Italy. Republic of Lebanon proclaimed.

1927—Stalin becomes Soviet dictator. Economic conference in Geneva attended by fifty-two nations.

1928—Herbert Hoover is elected president. U.S. and many other nations sign Kellogg-Briand pacts to outlaw war.

1929—Stock prices in New York crash on "Black Thursday"; the Great Depression begins.

1930—Bank of U.S. and its many branches close (most significant bank failure of the year). William Howard Taft dies in Washington, D.C.

1931—Emigration from U.S. exceeds immigration for first time as Depression deepens.

1932—Franklin D. Roosevelt wins presidential election in a Democratic landslide.

1933—First concentration camps are erected in Germany. U.S. recognizes USSR and resumes trade. Twenty-First Amendment repeals prohibition. Calvin Coolidge dies in Northampton, Massachusetts.

1934—Severe dust storms hit Plains states. President Roosevelt passes U.S. Social Security Act.

1936—Roosevelt is reelected. Spanish Civil War begins. Hitler and Mussolini form Rome-Berlin Axis.

1937—Roosevelt signs Neutrality Act.

1938—Roosevelt sends appeal to Hitler and Mussolini to settle European problems amicably.

1939—Germany takes over Czechoslovakia and invades Poland, starting World War II.

1940—Roosevelt is reelected for a third term.

1941—Japan bombs Pearl Harbor, U.S. declares war on Japan. Germany and Italy declare war on U.S.; U.S. then declares war on them.

1942—Allies agree not to make separate peace treaties with the enemies. U.S. government transfers more than 100,000 Nisei (Japanese-Americans) from west coast to inland concentration camps.

1943—Allied bombings of Germany begin.

1944—Roosevelt is reelected for a fourth term. Allied forces invade Normandy on D-Day.

1945—President Franklin D. Roosevelt dies in Warm Springs, Georgia; Vice-President Harry S. Truman succeeds him. Mussolini is killed; Hitler commits suicide. Germany surrenders. U.S. drops atomic bomb on Hiroshima; Japan surrenders: end of World War II.

1946—U.N. General Assembly holds its first session in London. Peace conference of twenty-one nations is held in Paris.

1947—Peace treaties are signed in Paris. "Cold War" is in full swing.

1948—U.S. passes Marshall Plan Act, providing $17 billion in aid for Europe. U.S. recognizes new nation of Israel. India and Pakistan become free of British rule. Truman is elected president.

1949—Republic of Eire is proclaimed in Dublin. Russia blocks land route access from Western Germany to Berlin; airlift begins. U.S., France, and Britain agree to merge their zones of occupation in West Germany. Apartheid program begins in South Africa.

1950—Riots in Johannesburg, South Africa, against apartheid. North Korea invades South Korea. U.N. forces land in South Korea and recapture Seoul.

1951—Twenty-Second Amendment limits president to two terms.

1952—Dwight D. Eisenhower resigns as supreme commander in Europe and is elected president.

1953—Stalin dies; struggle for power in Russia follows. Rosenbergs are executed for espionage.

1954—U.S. and Japan sign mutual defense agreement.

1955—Blacks in Montgomery, Alabama, boycott segregated bus lines.

1956—Eisenhower is reelected president. Soviet troops march into Hungary.

1957—U.S. agrees to withdraw ground forces from Japan. Russia launches first satellite, *Sputnik*.

1958—European Common Market comes into being. Alaska becomes the forty-ninth state. Fidel Castro begins war against Batista government in Cuba.

1959—Hawaii becomes fiftieth state. Castro becomes premier of Cuba. De Gaulle is proclaimed president of the Fifth Republic of France.

1960—Historic debates between Senator John F. Kennedy and Vice-President Richard Nixon are televised. Kennedy is elected president. Brezhnev becomes president of USSR.

1961—Berlin Wall is constructed. Kennedy and Khrushchev confer in Vienna. In Bay of Pigs incident, Cubans trained by CIA attempt to overthrow Castro.

1962—U.S. military council is established in South Vietnam.

1963—Riots and beatings by police and whites mark civil rights demonstrations in Birmingham, Alabama; 30,000 troops are called out, Martin Luther King, Jr., is arrested. Freedom marchers descend on Washington, D.C., to demonstrate. President Kennedy is assassinated in Dallas, Texas; Vice-President Lyndon B. Johnson is sworn in as president.

1964—U.S. aircraft bomb North Vietnam. Johnson is elected president. Herbert Hoover dies in New York City.

1965—U.S. combat troops arrive in South Vietnam.

1966—Thousands protest U.S. policy in Vietnam. National Guard quells race riots in Chicago.

1967—Six-Day War between Israel and Arab nations.

1968—Martin Luther King, Jr., is assassinated in Memphis, Tennessee. Senator Robert Kennedy is assassinated in Los Angeles. Riots and police brutality take place at Democratic National Convention in Chicago. Richard Nixon is elected president. Czechoslovakia is invaded by Soviet troops.

1969—Dwight D. Eisenhower dies in Washington, D.C. Hundreds of thousands of people in several U.S. cities demonstrate against Vietnam War.

1970—Four Vietnam War protesters are killed by National Guardsmen at Kent State University in Ohio.

1971—Twenty-Sixth Amendment allows eighteen-year-olds to vote.

1972—Nixon visits Communist China; is reelected president in near-record landslide. Watergate affair begins when five men are arrested in the Watergate hotel complex in Washington, D.C. Nixon announces resignations of aides Haldeman, Ehrlichman, and Dean and Attorney General Kleindienst as a result of Watergate-related charges. Harry S. Truman dies in Kansas City, Missouri.

1973—Vice-President Spiro Agnew resigns; Gerald Ford is named vice-president. Vietnam peace treaty is formally approved after nineteen months of negotiations. Lyndon B. Johnson dies in San Antonio, Texas.

1974—As a result of Watergate cover-up, impeachment is considered; Nixon resigns and Ford becomes president. Ford pardons Nixon and grants limited amnesty to Vietnam War draft evaders and military deserters.

1975—U.S. civilians are evacuated from Saigon, South Vietnam, as Communist forces complete takeover of South Vietnam.

1976—U.S. celebrates its Bicentennial. James Earl Carter becomes president.

1977—Carter pardons most Vietnam draft evaders, numbering some 10,000.

1980—Ronald Reagan is elected president.

1981—President Reagan is shot in the chest in assassination attempt. Sandra Day O'Connor is appointed first woman justice of the Supreme Court.

1983—U.S. troops invade island of Grenada.

1984—Reagan is reelected president. Democratic candidate Walter Mondale's running mate, Geraldine Ferraro, is the first woman selected for vice-president by a major U.S. political party.

1985—Soviet Communist Party secretary Konstantin Chernenko dies; Mikhail Gorbachev succeeds him. U.S. and Soviet officials discuss arms control in Geneva. Reagan and Gorbachev hold summit conference in Geneva. Racial tensions accelerate in South Africa.

1986—Space shuttle *Challenger* explodes shortly after takeoff; crew of seven dies. U.S. bombs bases in Libya. Corazon Aquino defeats Ferdinand Marcos in Philippine presidential election.

1987—Iraqi missile rips the U.S. frigate *Stark* in the Persian Gulf, killing thirty-seven American sailors. Congress holds hearings to investigate sale of U.S. arms to Iran to finance Nicaraguan *contra* movement.

Index

Page numbers in boldface type indicate illustrations.

About the Author

Zachary Kent grew up in Little Falls, New Jersey, and received an English degree from St. Lawrence University. Following college he worked at a New York City literary agency for two years and then launched his writing career. To support himself while writing, he has worked as a taxi driver, a shipping clerk, and a house painter. Mr. Kent has had a lifelong interest in American history. Studying the U.S. presidents was his childhood hobby. His collection of presidential items includes books, pictures, and games, as well as several autographed letters.